THE LONG CHRISTMAS RIDE HOME

A PUPPET PLAY WITH ACTORS

BY PAULA VOGEL

DRAMATISTS
PLAY SERVICE
INC.

THE LONG CHRISTMAS RIDE HOME
Copyright © 2004, Paula Vogel

All Rights Reserved

SPECIAL NOTE
Anyone receiving permission to produce THE LONG CHRISTMAS RIDE HOME is required to give credit to the Author as sole and exclusive Author of the Play on the title page of all programs distributed in connection with performances of the Play and in all instances in which the title of the Play appears for purposes of advertising, publicizing or otherwise exploiting the Play and/or a production thereof. The name of the Author must appear on a separate line, in which no other name appears, immediately beneath the title and in size of type equal to 50% of the size of the largest, most prominent letter used for the title of the Play. No person, firm or entity may receive credit larger or more prominent than that accorded the Author. The following acknowledgments must appear on the title page in all programs distributed in connection with performances of the Play and in all advertising and publicity in which full production credits appear:

THE LONG CHRISTMAS RIDE HOME received its New York premiere by the Vineyard Theatre, Douglas Aibel, Artistic Director, October 2003.

THE LONG CHRISTMAS RIDE HOME received its world premiere in a co-production by Long Wharf Theatre (Gordon Edelstein, Artistic Director) and Trinity Repertory Company (Oskar Eustis, Artistic Director; Edgar Dobie, Managing Director) in Providence, Rhode Island, opening in May 2003.

SPECIAL NOTE ON SONGS AND RECORDINGS
For performances of copyrighted songs, arrangements or recordings mentioned in this Play, the permission of the copyright owner(s) must be obtained. Other songs, arrangements or recordings may be substituted provided permission from the copyright owner(s) of such songs, arrangements or recordings is obtained; or songs, arrangements or recordings in the public domain may be substituted.

This play is dedicated to Mark Vogel.

AUTHOR'S NOTE

Thoughts on production:

Each year, I attend the Christmas Eve service at the Unitarian Universalist Church in Provincetown, Massachusetts, a town of 6,000 people, off-season. I mention this fact because, when I sat down to write this play, I did not have elaborate production values in mind. I wrote this play mindful of pageants that are performed in church basements and community halls. The play in my mind is closer to the church pageant in Jane Campion's film *The Piano* than, say, the pageantry of *The Lion King* on Broadway (although if one wants to produce this play on that budget, I am delighted). But what I am after is the magic we feel from communal participation in the make-believe of the spirit. Basil Twist, my master puppeteer, created such magic in 135 seats at the Vineyard, and the much larger Long Wharf Theatre, using silk and sticks. I urge directors to consult with puppeteers in town, or to create your own puppets. We used Punch and Judy–type puppets for the middle sections in Providence, and shadow puppetry in New York for the midsection. It is also possible to do the midsections as monologues.

With a few simple effects, each Christmas in Provincetown, by the light of candles we hold, we are transported by the story told in our community: When the chorus tackles *The Messiah*, it sounds like the Choir at Westminster Abbey to me.

Notes on the play:

This play is a fusion of a one-act and Bunraku puppet theatre techniques — or more importantly, of one westerner's misunderstanding of Bunraku. The misunderstanding is key.

The stage should be simple, elegant, bare. Short stools or chairs for the two narrators to one side of the stage. In the off-center stage, two rows of benches, with the back row elevated above the front — rather like bleachers.

If possible, it would be great to have a samisen player alongside of the narrators — playing Bunraku music, but also Christmas music adapted to the tonal scales of Bunraku.

Or a Hawaiian guitar. Or any string instrument — a steel guitar, a ukulele. A live player. Or not. Taped music. Perhaps a boom box beside the performers. Bells. Wooden clappers. Music and sound effects run under the entire play.

And if it is possible, the narrators and puppeteers can sing.

About the narrators:

One man. One woman. Age is not important. What matters is the sound of their voices: rich, sonorous voices capable of playing all genders, all ages, the sound of the snow, able to rise from a hush to crescendo. We could listen to them all night.

The minister/dancer:

We should not notice how young and beautiful he is until he dances.

The puppets:

The director must decide on what type of puppets represent the three children: Rebecca, the eldest, age 12; Stephen, the middle, age 9; and Claire, the youngest, age 7.

The puppets may be in the style of Bunraku: almost life-sized children. There is nothing cute or coy about the child puppets: They are fascinating and quite life-like in their animation. And they may be a little spooky, too — as anyone will tell you who has been caught in the stare of a puppet. These puppets may be manipulated by a single puppeteer. Other styles of puppets are possible. But if there are two or three puppeteers, we should feature the actor who will become the adult persona of the puppet child (if one uses Bunraku veils, the actors should be without veil).

The puppeteers:

They are actors, not professional puppeteers (can we add a week of rehearsal to the schedule?). They are dressed in black; their faces, while the puppets are center stage, are neutral and unemotive.

The actor who moves Rebecca should be a young woman in her late twenties to mid-thirties. Attractive, but careless in her appearance.

The actor who moves Claire should be in her mid-thirties; strong-looking, short-cropped hair. A woman one would not necessarily notice or look at, like the puppeteer behind the puppet.

The actor who moves Stephen should be in his late twenties to mid-thirties, thin, intelligent, mercurial of mood.

While the puppeteers wear black, the narrators and puppets are wearing their Sunday best.

I have read that Noh plays are always presented in the season they represent: spring, summer, winter and fall.

I suggest this play be produced in January, in October — in any month except December (although we played in a December blizzard in New York!). The before and the aftermath.

—Paula Vogel

THE LONG CHRISTMAS RIDE HOME received its world premiere in a co-production by Long Wharf Theatre (Gordon Edelstein, Artistic Director) and Trinity Repertory Company (Oskar Eustis, Artistic Director; Edgar Dobie, Managing Director) in Providence, Rhode Island, opening in May 2003. It was directed by Oskar Eustis; the set design was by Loy Arcenas; the lighting design was by Pat Collins; the sound design was by Darron L. West; the choreography was by Donna Uchizono; the costume design was by William Lane; the puppet design was by Basil Twist; and the stage manager was Jennifer Sturch. The cast was as follows:

MAN	Timothy Crowe
WOMAN	Anne Scurria
CLAIRE	Angela Brazil
REBECCA	Rachel Warren
STEPHEN	Stephen Thorne
MINISTER	Seán Martin Hingston
PUPPETEERS	Joshua Boggioni, Joanna Cole Virginia Eckert, Andy Gaukel Maya Para, Paul Ricciardi
MUSICIAN	Sumie Kaneko

THE LONG CHRISTMAS RIDE HOME premiered in New York City at the Vineyard Theatre (Douglas Aibel, Artistic Director; Bardo S. Ramirez, Managing Director; Jennifer Garvey-Blackwell, Executive Director/External Affairs), opening in October 2003. It was directed by Mark Brokaw; the set design was by Neil Patel; the lighting design was by Mark McCollough; the original music and sound design were by David Van Tieghem; the projections design was by Jan Hartley; the choreography was by John Carrafa; the costume design was by Jess Goldstein; the puppet design was by Basil Twist; and the production stage manager was Michael McGoff. The cast was as follows:

NARRATOR/MAN	Mark Blum
NARRATOR/WOMAN	Randy Graff
CLAIRE	Enid Graham
REBECCA	Catherine Kellner
STEPHEN	Will McCormack
MINISTER/DANCER	Sean Palmer
PUPPETEERS	Matthew Acheson, Oliver Dalzell Erin K. Orr, Mark Petrosino Sarah Provost, Lake Simons
MUSICIAN	Luke Notary

CHARACTERS

NARRATOR/MAN

NARRATOR/WOMAN

CLAIRE

REBECCA

STEPHEN

MINISTER/DANCER

FLOATING WORLD

For you, dear crew,
This thistle
Have you heard of One
One called Komache?
We float like seaweed
She has said,
Now tangle, next part.
But I say like thistle
Are we blown.
Things of the sea
Stop at the shore,
But things of the air
Roll on always.
For you, dear crew,
This thistle.

—Carl Vogel
(from an unpublished manuscript)

THE LONG CHRISTMAS RIDE HOME

Stephen enters. Beat. The two narrators enter and sit beside the musician. The three look at each other for a beat. They share a common breath. And then they commence:

GHOST of STEPHEN.

It was a very cold Christmas in a long and cold winter —
decades and days ago.

WOMAN.

On the outskirts of Washington, D.C.

Inside the Beltway.

MAN.

Concrete frozen with ice and stalled cars.

A cold winter —

WOMAN.

— It was not that cold. It was damp.

MAN.

It was freezing.

WOMAN.

I've gone through winters in New Orleans worse.

It's the damp that chills you.

MAN.

Colder than Times Square on New Year's.

Colder than the monuments on the mall.

Colder than Washingtonians at a cocktail party.

WOMAN.

It's the damp —

MAN.

It was *fucking* freezing *frigid*.

As Frigid as —

(A pause, a breath.)

WOMAN.

It was a cold Christmas that year.

(Breath.)

MAN.

On their way to the grandparents' apartment
The family of five inched their way along the surface roads
in a filthy Rambler.

(The puppeteers guide the children in: perhaps a miniature back seat of a car. Perhaps not. Throughout the opening car sequence, the puppets intermittently play stupid, silly, vicious children's games. Starting with Last Touch and escalating from there.)

WOMAN.

Father, mother, daughters and son.
The children hunched in the back,
Shivering and carsick. The wrapped presents
Piled in the trunk.

MAN.

The car smelled of stale cigarettes

WOMAN.

Cigarette smoke wafted on the currents of heat
Cranking from the Rambler's vents.

MAN.

The boy broke the silence first:
"Mama, I'm going to be sick."

WOMAN.

The father kept driving, lurching the car forward
With a right foot on the accelerator, a spastic,
Uneven tempo. The father grew up in Manhattan.
He would never learn to master the car.

MAN.

"Mama, I'm going to be sick."

WOMAN.

Christ! The father said. "How can he be sick?
He hasn't eaten today."

MAN.

The mother turned from her front seat, and with a practiced eye
Looked at the pallor of her son's skin.
With a critical eye, she appraised the frown,
The irritation on her husband's face.
Her husband had his good days and his bad days.
And today would be …

14

WOMAN.

"Open the window on your side. Breathe in the cold air."

(The Stephen puppet mimes opening the window.)

A sliver of ice and air rushed through the car.

The smell of damp wool coats,

the faint and sweet carsickness

from last summer's trip through the mountains

Ran out of the crack of the window.

MAN.

For a moment, the family breathed in deeply.

(All breathe.)

WOMAN.

Rebecca, the eldest, said to her brother Stephen

in a voice so low

It could not be heard in the front:

MAN.

"Don't breathe on me, Puke-Breath."

WOMAN.

And she accompanied it with a sharp jab.

MAN.

Stephen pressed up to the glass

And let the smooth chill caress his cheek.

WOMAN.

Claire, the youngest, chimed in next:

MAN.

"If you're gonna throw up, do it on

your clothes this time."

WOMAN.

The mother glanced at her husband.

"Ray? Maybe we should pull over."

MAN.

And in a voice too low to be heard in the back

Her husband muttered:

Maybe we should just go home.

WOMAN.

We go through this every year. Please.

It's Christmas.

MAN.

And Rebecca chorused from the back:

WOMAN.

"Mom? Daddy? He's gonna spew. Do I have to sit in the back

with these *children?*"

MAN.

Do you want me to stop or not?

We're late.

WOMAN.

Rebecca pleaded one more time:

"Can I please sit up front with you, Daddy?"

MAN.

No one responded in the front.

WOMAN.

And the father pressed on the pedal,

Rocking the car, skidding forward,

Right, then left, then back forward.

MAN.

The mother gripped the car seat.

Then she commanded:

WOMAN.

"Stephen: roll down the window

And stick your head out."

(The Stephen puppet hangs out of the window as the other two puppets draw away from him.)

And as they traveled, a Rambler piled with gifts,

The head of a small boy hanging from its side:

The rhythmic whip of tire chains on ice and snow

Made the children dance and

Lulled them into a Christmas reverie:

(A Christmas melody, punctuated with chain, jaunty. The puppet children dance in the back seat.)

MAN.

Rebecca, the eldest, thought of the red-faced boy

She would not see until school began.

She thought of the wisp of hair that hung in his eyes.

She thought of the bulge in his trousers she should not think of.

WOMAN.

And Claire thought of the turkey, browning in the oven,

She thought of the sliver of breast and thigh

Her grandfather would serve her

On her own china plate; Claire whispered the names

of all the food she would eat:

Cranberry, oyster dressing resplendent with sage and celery

MAN.

Gravy and mashed potatoes, onion and

WOMAN.

olive relish

and gravy and turkey and two kinds of pie:

(Hearing her, the Stephen puppet turns greener.)

As Claire's stomach ached

MAN.

His stomach ached, so Stephen tried not to think

Of the turkey, the thick, rich foods, the gravy, the onions, oh
   god,

He felt his gorge rising, he bit his lip, he tried to think of

Something else —

WOMAN.

Rebecca exploded in the back seat:

"Shut up!" And kicked her sister.

"He's going to toss all over me! Mom! Daddy!

Why do I have to be nursemaid to these children!

I want to sit up front!"

MAN.

Neither of her parents noticed.

WOMAN.

Think, Stephen, of something else:

He pictured the boys from school racing on the field.

It always made him happy and sad to watch them:

a blur of shorts and flesh and the spinning orb of the ball

the red-faced boys, the thin legs kicking

MAN.

And his stomach fluttered, his breath caught: dizzy,

He clutched the door. Was he bad? For watching boys?

Think, Stephen, of something else

Without heat and motion

WOMAN.

He thought of snow and ice and

snow and ice and snow

MAN.

And as they thought of the pleasures of the table,

the pleasures of the tree, the pleasures of the flesh:

The mother thought perhaps she should have an affair

To feel the heat and motion of a man's body against hers.

WOMAN.

And the father tried not to think of Sheila:

But did she like the cashmere?

Would she wear the silver and turquoise pendant,

swinging towards her breasts.

The cream of her breasts marking the brown of her skin

And the perfume he had bought?

When would he be able to breathe in the perfume

dabbled on the sliver of her thigh?

When could he see her? He must see her.

He must talk with her. He must Devour Her.

He could not sleep. Sheila. Sheila. Sheila. Sheila.

MAN.

And the mother said to her husband softly:

WOMAN.

"Penny for your thoughts."

The husband was startled to find his wife's hand

Nestled in his own.

He drew his hand back to the steering wheel:

MAN.

"Who can think in this family?"

And he said in a voice so low in the front seat

it could not be heard in the back

"I can't *breathe* in this family."

WOMAN.

"He must think I'm retarded.

Does he think I do not know?

Where he is on his so-called Business Trips?"

When she was a much younger wife

She had tracked her husband

To motel rooms where she would stand outside

the window while he consorted with his lovers inside.

She no longer followed his trail of evidence; who had the time?

He had slept with half the wives in the church —

Possibly the minister's wife herself! —

MAN.

And her husband said:

"I may need to visit a client tomorrow."

WOMAN.

And the mother smiled a thin, brittle smile.

MAN.

The man from the grocery last week had looked at her legs
When she turned to get the money; up and down her legs.
The children were out, her husband at work. How simple it
   would be
To lead him up the stairs, put his hands on her breasts,
Plunge her hands down his trousers,
And tumble onto the bed she made up every morning:
And in the aftermath, as he pulled on his pants he might say:

WOMAN.

"Lady, your husband's a fool."

MAN.

And Claire rocked in anticipation of the gifts.
Would she find what she had asked for
Under the tree today?

WOMAN.

She had asked for cowboy boots and cowboy guns;
Blazing six-shooters to conquer the West

(Claire draws imaginary guns and conquers an imaginary West.)

She had not noticed that slight crease
in her mother's brow, a concern,
A question too soon to be asked.

MAN.

And the mother thought:
He's in deep this time. The mother knew
Exactly who she was; the new woman in church: Sheila Jackson.
With a husband and a daughter and a hearth of her own.
She wondered if her husband had money left over
from the gifts her husband had bestowed

WOMAN.

On That Woman.

MAN.

Jewish men

WOMAN.

Love their children, invest their money, never drink

MAN.

Jewish men

WOMAN.

Obey the ninth commandment,
Revere their shiksa wives.
Of all the Jewish men in the world

She had to marry this one
MAN.

The mother sighed, and her breath frosted the window.
WOMAN.

"I should get pregnant again. Perhaps another child
Will end this infatuation. Surely he would not leave me then."
MAN.

And the chains called out the rhyme and the melody
WOMAN.

And the father thought when would he be able to breathe in
the perfume
MAN.

And Rebecca thought when could she call the boy at school
WOMAN.

And the mother thought tomorrow night would be a good
time to try
MAN.

And Stephen never wondered what lay in the brightly colored
Boxes in the trunk, the presents and ribbons under the tree
Because he already knew what each held inside:
disappointment.
(Stagehands bear miniature trees, wreaths, reindeer across the stage.)
But it smelled like Christmas on the air.
It was that time again. Christmas day was passing into night.
The light had left the sky early, and he forgot his sickness.
Stephen watched the lights of other Christmas trees in other
houses
Flashing by.
WOMAN.

Icicles edged the gutters,
While reindeer raced across suburban lawns.
The house on the corner blinked, blinked, blinked, blinked.
MAN.

Stephen's thoughts returned to last night; the lights and music in
the church.
*(The puppets exit the car and promenade in a circle around the stage,
to another part: The Unitarian Universalist Church.)*
WOMAN.

Christmas Eve at the Unitarian Universalist Church of Rock
Springs.
The family entered the church together in a flock.

As they drew off their coats, the mother spied the Jackson family.

MAN.

Hearty smiles were exchanged across the room; the

Adulterer and the cuckold; the martyred and the married.

MAN and WOMAN.

"Merry Christmas!"

WOMAN.

"Ray?!"

MAN.

"Bob!"

WOMAN.

"Sheila! Susy!"

MAN.

"Kate! Kids!"

Only Stephen noticed his mother stiffen.

He took her side.

WOMAN.

"You look beautiful tonight, Mama."

MAN.

Stephen said.

WOMAN.

And that is how the term "Mama's boy" got made.

MAN.

The mother smiled, and pressed her son, her only boy

To her side.

WOMAN.

Other families crowded in the vestibule.

Husbands exerted slight and subtle pressure on their wives' arms

To steer them away from their father, Ray. A coolness in the greetings

That sang across the vestibule:

MAN.

"Merry Christmas, Ray. Kate. To all."

WOMAN.

"Merry Christmas!"

MAN.

"Merry Christmas!

WOMAN and MAN.

"Merry Christmas!"

(The puppets bow, curtsy, to other families. Jab each other. The puppets sit in the pew.)

MAN.

Shh! The service is beginning!

*(Christmas music, in the tonality of Bunraku, begins. Another actor
enters wearing a clerical collar.)*

MINISTER.

Welcome all, to our Christmas Evening service.

I am honored to spend this, my family's first Christmas
back home from Japan,

here with you at the Unitarian Universalist Church
of Rock Springs.

I am honored to serve you until your own minister

Recovers — ah, returns — from his sabbatical.

We send him and his family

Holiday greetings, holiday wishes. Thoughts of peace.

As your minister tonight, as we celebrate the most spiritual
Night of the West,

I thought I would share with you

The beauty of Japan, the peace of the East

(The puppet children stir.)

MAN.

And the man muttered low to his wife

"Oi! Ba-ruch a-tah A-do-nai E-lo-hei-nu, Me-lech Ha-o-lam."

WOMAN.

And she responded "Hail-Mary-Mother-of-God-Blessed-is-
the-Fruit-of-thy-Womb-Jesus"

And the two twittered in a secret joke shared

Only between lapsed Catholics

MAN.

and Assimilated Jews

MAN and WOMAN.

On a pew in the Unitarian Universalist Church.

MAN.

And Claire said, in a loud whisper:

"Aren't we going to sing carols?"

(As the father.)

Shhh!

MINISTER.

I was struck by how akin the great works of Japan

Are to our Renaissance Nativity scenes — the same Great Spirit

That captures the Mother and Child in the manger

Infuses the woodblocks of Edo.

MAN.
(As Claire.)

"I wanna sing carols!"
(As the father.)

Shhh!

MINISTER.

And surely we, as Unitarians, recognize the spirit of the divine
In every land and every tongue.
Before I share slides with you of these beautiful works from Japan,
Let us rise and offer up our voices together.
In the hymnal in front of you: "Good King Wenceslas"

MAN.

And as the congregation rose to their feet
And shuffled through the hymnal,
Their father spied his love across the room.
"When oh when will I be able to talk to you again?
I must see you. I must see you."
His beloved gave an imperceptible nod of her head,
Then quickly Sheila Jackson smiled at her daughter, hugging her.
A picture of the perfect mother.
The father looked at his wife and thought: O God help me.

ALL.
(Singing.)

Good King Wenceslas looked out
On the Feast of Stephen

MAN.

And their mother Kate caught a glimpse
Of this perfect picture of her rival
Angelically singing beside Mr. Jackson
And their mother thought:
"Look at her hands, look at her neck.
Oh Christ, she looks ten years younger."

ALL.

When the snow lay round about
Deep and Crisp and Even.

MAN.

And the eldest child Rebecca looked at the pitiful pock-faced
   boys
In the pews around her.
Why did they have to be Uni-Unis? Why couldn't they be
   Catholic?

Catholic Boys served at the Altar;
Catholic Boys were guilty —
Catholic Boys were hot ...
ALL.
Brightly shone the moon that night
Though the frost was cruel
MAN.
And the littlest one whispered:
"What do we believe?
Is Christ the King? What's Redeemer mean?
Does Christ Rise like Bread? What's the feast of Stephen?"
"Later," her mother groaned.
"But what do we believe?"
"Shh!" Her father said.
ALL.
(Singing.)
Sire the night is darker now,
And the wind blows stronger
Fails my heart, I know not how
I can go no longer ...
(All hum underneath.)
MAN.
"Oh Sheila. My love. My Sheila. When?"
WOMAN.
"I am getting old. He does not love me."
MAN.
(As Rebecca.)
"Catholic boys are hot."
WOMAN.
(As Stephen.)
"You look beautiful tonight, Mama."
MAN.
(As Claire.)
"But What Do We Believe?"
(The minister beckons the congregation to sit. The minister shows slides. There is a slide show — or not.)
MINISTER.
Please be seated. May I have the first slide?
Tonight I want to talk to you about the spirit and the flesh.
And to help us look at these questions of faith, I want to turn to
The woodblock prints of Japan.

Sometimes using the distance and perspective
Of a Far-off land, of another people
We can return and see our home more clearly.
MAN.
"Oi."
MINISTER.
Buddha taught us that the world
And all its joys are fleeting, too soon melted away.
But rather than renounce the joys of this world:
The pleasures of the flesh, the joy in watching
The heat and motion of the flesh,
MAN.
— Where did they find this guy?
MINISTER.
The tastes and temptations of the flesh —
These artists and courtesans, actors and merchants
Determined to enjoy the flesh because it was ephemeral.
Putting aside Western notions of guilt and shame about the
    body —
Why not embrace what will too soon be gone?
(The Stephen puppet leans forward in his seat, listening intently.)
These few slides represent the art of the Edo period
In Japan. Artists who wrestled with this relationship of man
And nature called this art: "Ukiyo-e"
The Floating World.
WOMAN.
Quietly, so no one else would hear
Stephen repeated to himself in a whisper:
"Ukiyo-e"
MINISTER.
Ukiyo-e. The Floating World.
MAN.
"Christ! Is this a museum or a church?"
MINISTER.
It is not only Joy To The World! It is Joy In the World!
MAN.
Oi!
MINISTER.
In the same way we, on this Christmas Eve, embrace
Our hearth and our home, share the pleasures of the table

WOMAN.

    — "Please God, and the bed — "

MINISTER.

    Celebrate the eternal made flesh! In a lowly manger —

    Savor the image of the mother and child because of

    His brief stay with us on earth —

    — More slides please —

MAN.

    And the minister showed paintings of Mount Fuji

    Encrusted with snow — dwarfing the tiny figures of man.

    Brush strokes of Cherry Blossoms, lovely for a day.

    He talked about the weather and the winds

    And how we as mortals bow to these tides of the earth

MINISTER.

    — All reflected in the pen and the brush of the floating world.

WOMAN.

    And Stephen whispered: "Ukiyo-e"

MINISTER.

    The minister continued, unmindful of the rustling snickers

    Of the Washingtonians in his pews.

    He showed fantastic things! —

WOMAN.

                         — parallel lines that

    Recede and draw us into the canvas of the floating world:

    Artists celebrating the everyday world of commoners,

    The beauty in the commonplace —

(Suddenly a slide flashes of a Japanese Prostitute.)

MINISTER.

    — Ooops.

    Sorry. This wasn't supposed to be — well. No harm done.

    As you can see, this is a picture of a lady of the ... um,

    Theater district of Edo. A working lady.

    And on top a very nice gentleman, possibly of the warrior class.

    In our culture, we revere Mary Magdalene in a similar way.

    Although Mary Magdalene, um, renounced her line of work.

MAN.

    The snickers of the adults grew into breaths of laughter.

WOMAN.

    And Claire asked: "Why are we laughing?"

(As Mother.)

    — Shhh!

And Claire asked:

"Did the Virgin Mary work?"

(As Mother.)

Shhh! No. She stayed at home. Like your mother.

(A breath.)

Sheila Jackson *works.*

(The minister smiles, acknowledging the laughter.)

MINISTER.

Yes, well. But while we're here — look at how
Lovely she is, this um, courtesan, this woman
How lovely in her brief time and place.

MAN.

And Stephen turned to his mother:

WOMAN.

"Oh! She looks beautiful, Mama."
And Stephen thought he had never seen
Anyone as beautiful as she. He would remember
The beauty of this woman, of this woodblock,
Of this night, for a long long time.

MINISTER.

Let us not judge on this night. Let us embrace
The Here and Now.

MINISTER, MAN and WOMAN.

We are all in this Floating World together.

WOMAN.

And then the most magical moment of all:
To music and dance, the minister presented:
The smallest of children in the congregation
Dressed in kimonos he had brought from Japan:
Bearing lanterns and silk, the little ones processed:
And created the crèche; a manger, and Mary,
And Joseph, oxen and lamb, wise men and stars,
And the baby Jesus swaddled in the most beautiful silk of all.

*(Stagehands, puppets, create a nativity scene in a dance; the arrival of
a pregnant Mary and Joseph in the manger; the journey of the Wise
Men; the birth of the Christ child, the gifts of the Magi and the adoration of the Christ child — who by his bouncing foot then leads them
all, animals and kings, into a rollicking dance.)*

The laughter subsided. The adults became children too,
And all danced and sang and fell silent.

ALL.

Oooohhhh …

(The nativity vanishes. A breath. The Man and Woman, puppets and puppeteers troop back to the car.)

WOMAN.

And on the way to the car after the service, Claire asked:

MAN.

"Do we believe in Buddha? Who is Buddha? What do we believe in?"

WOMAN.

"Unitarian Universalists are nondenominational. Which means When you are Older, you will decide for yourself what you believe in."

MAN.

"But why are we Unitarian — U — "

WOMAN.

— Because your father was raised Jewish. Your mother was raised Catholic.

We wanted a church for children from an intermarriage.

MAN.

"What is intermarriage?"

The family had reached the car, and climbed in. And right before The engine started, the father answered:

"Intermarriage is the mingling of blood from two cultures at war."

WOMAN.

Stephen heard none of his family that Christmas Eve, or during the trip the day after.

He pressed his forehead to the window glass

and saw beyond his reflection

Swirling kimonos, Cherry Blossoms, lovely for a day

MAN.

Wise Men and Stars, Lanterns and Silk

Mount Fuji encrusted in Winter Snow

WOMAN.

Boys kicking spinning orbs,

Courtesans and Courtiers

The strange music of

MAN and WOMAN.

The Floating World.

WOMAN.

Stephen's reverie was stopped by the crunching

28

Of ice beneath the car. They had arrived at
The grandparents' apartment: plain red-bricked
Boxes, cramped, identical and cheap.

MAN.

In a moment the family had jumped out.
Arms laden with gifts, they entered
The hallway. The smells of Grandmother's cooking
Greeted them from the doorway.

(The Minister joins the other narrators.)

MINISTER.

(As Grandmother.)

Ding-dong!

WOMAN.

And the door opened, and Grandmother was there,
In a flurry of wet coats and wrappings.

MINISTER.

(As Grandmother.)

Merry Christmas!

(The puppet children bow.)

WOMAN.

And they echoed glad tidings and hugged.
Their father drew back by the doorway.

MAN.

I could use a drink. Ho ho ho.

WOMAN.

And the grandfather brought out the scotch
And the bourbon

MINISTER.

(As Grandfather.)

Ho ho ho.

WOMAN.

The children drank eggnog.

(The puppets sit and are given small boxes.)

MINISTER.

And they sat around the tree to unwrap the gifts
while they drank, and the turkey browned, and
the ice in the drinks melted.

*(Stagehands rip large quantities of paper, amplified by microphone.
The bits of paper remain on the floor.)*

And the scotch and the bourbon were replenished.
Grandmother handed out her gifts to the children first.

29

(More paper-ripping sounds: Stagehands rip the wrapping/confetti on stage. As grandmother:)

    I hope you like these. I hope these fit. I found them
    in the trash room.

MAN.

    All the gifts from the grandparents were recycled from
    the trash room. It was their greatest pleasure
    Sifting through their neighbors' garbage.

MINISTER.

(As grandfather.)

    Well, when you've lived through the Depression,
    You know how to make use of what you have
    And what you find.

WOMAN.

    And the father said, "Christ" under his breath.

MAN.

    And replenished his drink.

    Straight up without ice.

(Stagehands drape a scarf around the Rebecca puppet.)

MINISTER.

(As grandmother.)

    I found this perfectly good scarf on top of the bags.
    And in such a cold winter! There was a stain — I'm not
    Quite sure what it was — it smelled a little — well —
    I washed it several times.
    You can barely see the stain.
    That scarf cost good money.

MAN.

    And the mother gave a careful look to her daughter.
    Who took the cue:

REBECCA.

(As young Rebecca.)

    Thank you, Grandmother, Rebecca said.

(The Rebecca puppet bows. Stagehands present mittens to the Claire puppet.)

MINISTER.

(As grandmother.)

    Those young people in 4D threw away
    These perfectly good mittens. Well, someone had snipped off
    All the fingertips and I started to darn them, but then I
        thought:

Isn't that clever! Your hands stay warm while your fingers can do all
sorts of things and — I hope they fit! It's amazing what
people throw away!

(The Claire puppet bows.)

CLAIRE.

(As young Claire.)

And Claire said, "Thank you, Grandmother."

(Stagehands put a wool cap on Stephen.)

MINISTER.

(As Grandmother.)

That should fit tight and snug! There was a
hole in the back — perfectly round, as if someone
pushed a stick through it — or a .22 caliber slug —

(The Stephen puppet bows.)

STEPHEN.

(As young Stephen.)

"Thank you, Grandmother."

MINISTER.

(As grandmother.)

Isn't it amazing what people throw away!

MAN.

And the grandfather replenished his drink. And poured another
For his son-in-law. The two men nodded at each other.

*(The puppet children begin to jab each other, play Last Touch, pretend-
pick their puppet noses and wipe it on each other. Whenever one of the
narrators look at them, they angelically bow. Rebecca tries to strangle
Stephen with her scarf.)*

WOMAN.

Kids. Stop it.

(She smiles.)

They're hungry: we've been saving our appetites!

MINISTER.

And the children played, and jabbed, and strangled each
other quietly while the parents opened their boxes.

WOMAN.

Kids.

MINISTER.

They did not notice or remember the adult gifts: expensive
gifts, store-bought for the grandparents by their mother.
Who had saved all year from the housekeeping allowance.

WOMAN.

    Kids!! ... and their father gave their mother a vacuum cleaner.
    Because, he said, she was so good at cleaning up their crap.
    No one laughed but the mother, who pretended it was
    Just what she'd hoped for! An Electrolux! Thank you —

MINISTER.

    And the grandmother said:
    "Oh, those are the best vacuums. I still
    have the one I found in the trash room.
    It was just missing a belt, and your father
    fixed it ... "

MAN.

    And they all replenished their drinks.
    And then the father handed out one box
    To each of his children:

(The Rebecca puppet opens her box.)

REBECCA.

    Rebecca got a leather diary. She smiled bravely.
    And thanked her parents. Who had already turned
    Their attention to their drinks; her mother watched Stephen;
    Her father watched Claire
    And Rebecca went unnoticed.
    Piss. She thought. By tomorrow night Stephen and Claire
    will have broken the lock and read everything I've written.

(The other puppets wrestle the diary away and read it.)

    And what do I have to write in my boring life?
    "Dear Diary: Today is Friday. What happened today?
        Nothing.
    Dear Diary. It's Saturday. Nothing happened today. Dear
        Diary:
    It's Christmas! And what happened today?"

(Two stagehands enter and deftly kick a soccer ball across the stage.)

STEPHEN.

    And Stephen unwrapped his gift:
    it was a soccer ball. For a boy who could barely run;
    Who was never chosen for teams, who only watched
    The red-faced boys kick and run down the field and
    parking lots. He would give the ball to his sisters and
    Watch them play.

(The Stephen puppet bows.)

    "Thank you, Father"

WOMAN.
>And then the father gave a small box
>Wrapped in silver to his youngest child.
>The other two pressed to see Claire unwrap it.

MINISTER.
>Yesterday in the jewelry store, when he bought
>Silver earrings for Sheila; silver rings, too:
>A silver bracelet, thick for her tapered wrist:
>As he ran towards the counter, in a frenzy
>Thinking of the silver against her skin:

WOMAN.
>And he thought:

MAN.
>Screw!

WOMAN.
>The rent for January.

MAN.
>Screw!

WOMAN.
>The grocery bill.

MAN.
>Screw!

WOMAN.
>The money for braces.

MAN.
>Screw!

WOMAN.
>The milkman, the doctor, the broken washing machine:
>The payment on the car, the savings for the house:

MAN.
>Screw! Wearing a tie and smiling for assholes
>and the hour commute:

WOMAN.
>He would buy the turquoise pendant too. Screw it all.

MAN.
>But he saw in the counter case
>A glint of gold.
>It was a delicate strand, almost gossamer:
>A bracelet for a child with three tiny charms:
>A little lock with a tiny key, a little house, and a little cowboy
>>gun.

WOMAN.

There went the electric bill.

MAN.

He would give it to Claire.

CLAIRE.

And Claire, who had been eyeing the soccer ball,
Suddenly stopped when she saw the desire
On her sister's face.
She saw the desire on her mother's face.
She saw a softness on her brother's face.
And they all breathed a soft:

ALL.

Ohhh.

MINISTER.

It was beautiful. It was gold.

WOMAN.

And the father knelt by his golden girl
And said:

MAN.

Each Christmas that we are together
I will give you one golden charm.

(The Claire puppet bows.)

CLAIRE.

And Claire gave her father a kiss.

MINISTER.

And the adults retreated into the dining room
And replenished their drinks.

WOMAN.

Grandfather sharpened his carving knife;
the women set the table with crystal and silver.
And the children played on their own.

MAN.

And somehow the men started talking

WOMAN.

Always a bad idea.

MAN.

And the talk ran to money, and how hard it was
To put food on the table for a family of five

MINISTER.

And the grandfather snorted, and talked about
Discipline. And saving. And tightening one's belt.

WOMAN.

And the grandmother tried to change the subject.

MAN.

And the talk ran to work, and salaries

And how much more the father earned

MINISTER.

Than the grandfather would see in a year

And where did the money go?

If the grandfather had his son-in-law's wages

He would have a mortgage

A house of his own

And the father said:

MAN.

Three children!

And the grandfather said:

MINISTER.

You shouldn't have more children

Than you can take care of —

MAN.

And the father laughed, a strangled laugh:

What's done cannot be undone

WOMAN.

And the mother tried to get her husband to help her.

STEPHEN.

And Stephen said to his sister:

"Let me wear the bracelet. For a moment."

(The two puppets start to struggle.)

CLAIRE.

And suddenly Claire wanted that bracelet

Around her wrist.

Play with your ball, she said.

WOMAN.

And the children didn't hear the voices

Change in the dining room

Nor a sudden silence of the women in the kitchen.

REBECCA.

And Rebecca said

"Oh let him wear it for a second."

WOMAN.

And suddenly there was a hush to the anger

in the men's voices:

MAN.

"I don't need you telling me how to run my own — "

MINISTER.

"What good is telling you anything?!"

MAN.

"We're paying back the money you loaned us — "

MINISTER.

"Damn right. You just throw money away — "

CLAIRE.

And Stephen grabbed Claire's wrist

STEPHEN.

Stephen did not grab Claire's wrist.

When Stephen touched the bracelet, Claire twisted away —

WOMAN.	CLAIRE.
And Claire said	"Get off — "
	REBECCA.
And Rebecca said	"You little toad"
	STEPHEN.
And Stephen said	"Just for a second"

WOMAN.

And they tugged and they turned.

And the fragile links of the golden bracelet twisted

And turned, stretched and strained

And the thin golden strand

Broke.

(A single metallic pluck of the samisen.)

For a moment the children stood still.

They had never broken anything golden before.

CLAIRE.

And Claire started crying.

STEPHEN.

And Stephen trembled where he stood.

REBECCA.

And Claire flew to her father.

CLAIRE.

"Daddy! Can you fix this?"

WOMAN.

The two men stopped their soft hissing.

The father drew his lips tight together:

And very very softly said:

MAN.

"How did this happen:"

CLAIRE.

"Stephen. He was just trying to — "

MAN.

— "Christ!"

He turned to his son.

"Get your coat on and get your little Pansy Ass out to the car.

No dinner for you. You are to wait until we are done."

And as if kicking a soccer ball, the father kicked at his son.

WOMAN.

And the women started in a chorus:

but the grandfather's baritone thundered through:

MINISTER.

"You will not send my grandson out in the cold.

Not on Christmas day."

MAN.

"He is my son and he will do what I tell him.

Get your fucking coat and"

WOMAN.

"And — "

MINISTER.

— And the grandfather reached down

And grabbed his son-in-law's shirt:

"You can treat my daughter like a dog if you will.

She is your wife.

But you will not kick my grandson — "

WOMAN.

And in a flash, the grandfather cried:

MINISTER.

"Kike!"

WOMAN.

And the father cried:

MAN.

"Cocksucker!"

MINISTER.

— And

MAN.

— And

WOMAN.

— And it happened! How could it possibly happen!

The two men waltzed in a wrestler's embrace:
the women grasping
MAN.

Shirt,
MINISTER.

Sleeve,
WOMAN.

Hair!
Trying to get between them,
MAN.

ripping cloth and collar
MINISTER.

And the men kicked
MAN.

And punched
MINISTER.

And crashed onto the table,
WOMAN.

shattering the crystal and clanging the silver
As the children scattered themselves and hid
(The puppets crouch protectively.)
MINISTER.
(As grandfather.)

Out of my house!
MAN.

And the mother sobbed:
WOMAN.

quick, children, grab the presents,
quick, children, grab your coats:
quick, children, grab your sister:
(The stagehands collect the presents.)
MAN.
(As father.)

We're leaving!
MINISTER.

And the women and children keened a collective:
ALL.

"Aaaahhhhh — !"
MINISTER.

And the family landed in the hall.
With the door slamming behind them.

For one stunned moment, no one moved.
The hallway echoed with Christmas music
From apartment 2D.
And the father said:

MAN.

"Get in the goddamned car."

(The minister exits. The narrators and puppets walk to the two benches. The man and woman sit on the front bench; the children and puppeteers climb up onto the back bench.)

The night was blue with cold.

WOMAN.

Black air on blue snow.
The wind threw them back as they rushed to the car.
The Trunk was thrown open
And the Gifts were thrown in:

MAN.

A Soccer ball, a diary, an Electrolux,
Crap! Thrown away by strangers —
The Trunk slammed shut.
Four doors encased in ice were pried open
Four door slams.

(Wooden percussion. The Minister enters and narrates:)

MINISTER.

The sound of chain and wheel on snow-encrusted ice:
A whinny of metal, a spinning of rubber
And the car lurched away from the curb
And spun into the night.
No one spoke inside the car.
Rebecca thought of what she would write in her diary tonight.

REBECCA.

She would write:
"Dear Diary: I hate my sister. I hate my family. I hate my life."
And she would write how much she hated ugly words
Words with a hard K-uh consonant:
Words like:

MAN.

"K-ike"

MINISTER.

And

WOMAN.

"K-ock. Su-ck"

MAN, WOMAN and REBECCA.
"And Christmas."
REBECCA.

And in the hush of the back seat
Rebecca turned to her little sister and said
In a voice so low it could not be heard in the front
"This is all your fault."

WOMAN.

And Claire sat in the back: feeling the shame.
The shame of being the golden girl. It was her fault. All of it.
And whatever happened from that moment on
Moments linked to moments
It was all her fault.

MINISTER.

And unable to grasp the enormity of that shame
In her seven-year-old mind: Claire thought instead of kites.

CLAIRE.

Why did her grandfather call her father a Kite?

(Two stagehands come in, flying kites. One small kite is given to the puppet.)

Why are kites bad? Was she bad? For flying kites?
How could kites be dirty?

(The puppet Claire lets go of her kite and watches it float away from the car.)

MINISTER.

And Stephen made himself very small.

STEPHEN.

He knew something had been named; something
that had to do with him … was he bad? For watching boys?
And he thought of his father: "He does not love me.
He does not love me. Why does he not love me?"

(The puppet Stephen draws his sleeve across his eyes.)

He wet his sleeve with tears.

MAN.

The only sound was the whir and clack of the wheels
The wipers' rhythmic percussion.
And a deeper silence within the car.
The silence skaters hear on the pond
Right before the dreadful cracking of ice.

MINISTER.

The mother pressed herself against the window.

There was a sigh.

What's done cannot be undone.

And then she broke the silence:

WOMAN.

"Well. What a lovely Christmas you've given me."

MINISTER.

And the father drew back his right hand:

MAN.

Je-Sus-Christt!

(The Man ritualistically draws his right hand back to strike:)

MINISTER.

The slashing of his hand through the air

Took an eternity

As the children froze in the back seat of the car

And Rebecca closed her eyes and vowed:

REBECCA.

"I will never have children!"

(The woodblocks, or stick drum, beat. In the crash of percussion, the puppeteer rises with the puppet of Rebecca: The two rip apart. A chrysalis bursting open: the adult Rebecca emerges from the car. Loud Japanese rock music plays. Rebecca, disheveled, half lurches, half dances, towards a door, towards her future, twenty-five years from the moment in the car we have just witnessed. Rebecca calls up to a window.)

Chester! Chester! What are you doin' home? Hey Chester — My keys aren't working in the lock! Come on down an' let me in, it is fucking freezing frigid. Chester! I'm down here on the street —

(A puppet appears, in a puppet fury. Question from the puppet.)

When was I going to tell you what?

(The puppet calls out.)

Did you read my Mail?!

(Puppet affirms "damn fucking right I read your mail.")

Okay. So I'm pregnant. Shit happens. I was gonna tell you when you got back home — Congratulations! Now let me in the goddamn door. The mother of your whatever-it-is is freezing to death out here.

(Chester waves his arms, yells.)

I had a drink with the girls at Toppers! A little Christmas ho ho ho — I had One little drink!

(To herself.)

An' about five little chasers ... I'm not keeping it anyway ...

(Chester throws out an expletive.)

What are you calling me?!

(More puppet threats.)

You always were a son of a bitch with math. So you were out of town on a business trip three months ago — wait a minute — did you go through my Diary? Did you? Did You Read My — !?

(The puppet yells, stamps, demands.)

Okay, okay! The "R" in my Diary stands for Rick.

(Puppet grabs his heart. Puppet goes berserk. He throws clothing, furniture, beats the walls. Huge Puppet rage.)

Chester! Chester! For god's sake — STOP!

Chester — honey — unlock the door, let me in, and I'll pack a bag.

(Puppet questions.)

I don't know where I'm going this time of the night. It's too late to go to my mother's. Do Not Call My Mother, Chester. She's upset already this time of year. I mean it. Don't you dare call Mom. I don't want to ruin her Christmas. And forget my bunking in with Claire she thinks the sun shines out your ass ... I could sleep on the couch tonight. I'll be gone in the morning.

(Puppet questions.)

Why? Why? I don't know why! Because ... because. When you're not here ... I need to be noticed.

(Chester puppet weeps.)

Oh Baby. Don't cry, baby. Come on, Chester, let me in.

(Chester puppet raises his head.)

You want me to keep the baby? You want us to raise it together — I don't think that's a good idea.

(Chester puppet kneels and proposes. Rebecca stiffens.)

You want me to marry you?

(Another proposal.)

We could call him *Stephen?* Or *Stephanie* if it's a girl!? Don't you dare fucking manipulate me by using my brother! No one is going to replace my brother. Ever! I hate feeling this baby using me like some *host* body —

(Chester puppet pleads from the window.)

No! I am not playing nursemaid to children! Great. I'll come by tomorrow when you're at work and pack up — or — no no — Screw it all.

You go boy! I don't care! Just throw out all my shit with the trash —

(Puppet hurls out an expletive.)

Oh Screw You, Chester! You son of a bitch — that's ...

pathetic! You change the locks, and now you want to raise his bas-
tard child?! A real man would come down here and slap the crap
out of —
(Chester puppet yells.)
— You're warning me? Chester!! You don't have the balls!
*(The little Puppet cuckold slams the window shut. Beat. Rebecca stands
in the silence. She laughs, sings.)*
"Have yourself a Merry little Christmas … "
Shit. You'd think I'd know by now not to leave my Diary lying
around …
Oh boy. I've got to sleep it off in the back seat of the car …
where the hell did I park the car … blocks and blocks away …
Christ it's cold. They're sayin' on the radio not to let your dogs and
cats out tonight … I gotta get off the street … I'm not going to
think about this right now. Just find the car. I've had practice not
thinking about stuff in a room at the Holiday Inn … There's so
much not to think about … you have to not to think about the
green paisley of the bedspread …
I think I parked down this block …
(Rebecca reaches where the car should be.)
Damn … This doesn't look familiar. Think, Rebecca. Maybe it's
the next block down — Oh, Jesus, I need to lie down. Wish I were
at the Holiday Inn, The Comfort Inn, the goddamned Dollar Inn.
(She continues to walk, very haltingly.)
Turn down the next block —
(She walks some more.)
And who the hell picks out the pattern for their headboards?
(She trails off. Looks around.)
Shit. This isn't right. It's the other way.
(She stumbles on.)
And then you have to concentrate on feeling the weight of his
thighs so you won't think about his wife waiting at home, the kids
listening for his key in the … So many things not to think about …
God, Rebecca, you just threw it all away.
(Rebecca stops, completely lost. The wind turns.)
I'm not gonna make it to the car. I've got to sleep. Now … Oh
look …
(Stagehands have brought out a bench.)
That snowdrift looks like the cleanest sheets I've ever seen … A
four-star hotel! Room Service! They've turned down the sheets …
(Rebecca lowers herself onto the "drift" and curls up. She removes her

scarf and bunches it up to form a pillow. She speaks to her stomach.)

It's funny — It's so cold you can really see your breath, but I don't feel cold at all … just very sleepy. We're gonna curl up together, all snug and warm, and … just … fall …

(Rebecca is out cold on the bench. In a dim light, a shadow is cast across the sleeping sister on the bench, and then we can make out the grown Stephen, standing, watching. Suddenly there is an eerie sound: an amplified breath prolonged, plaintive, that ends as a moan of winter wind. Rebecca's eyes, startled, open with a start. She sits up quickly.)

Stephen?!

(Only the wind answers her back. She stands, shivering like a sick dog, and runs. Stops. Wraps her coat tightly around her. Wide awake now:)

I have to find the car.

(And then she turns, quickens her steps, and leaves to look for shelter, for warmth, for a bed. Stephen watches her go. Beat.)

STEPHEN.

And in the car as our father drew back his right hand:

WOMAN.

Well, what a lovely Christmas you've given me.

(The man repeats his action, draws back his hand to strike his wife.)

CLAIRE.

If I had let Stephen wear it. If I hadn't yanked it away. If I had tried to fix it myself. If I'd made it into a joke. If I hadn't run to Daddy —

MAN.

Jesus — Christ!

CLAIRE.

"If, If, If, If, If … "

(The woodblocks/percussion beat again as the puppeteer holding Claire rises; she strips off the puppet and rises from the car. She walks to an apartment door upstage. It is twenty-four years in the future. She presses an intercom buzzer and speaks into a speaker.)

Naomi? Naomi. Naomi. Naomi. Come on, answer. I saw you go in. Naomi. Naomi.

Naomi? Naomi? I'm going to play "Jingle Bells" on the buzzer until you let me in —

"Dashing through the snow; in a one-horse open sleigh — o'er the fields we go — laughing all the way — Ha! Ha! Ha!"

(Suddenly the gaiety is gone; Claire slumps for a moment. Then she steps out onto the street.)

They won't answer the intercom. That's not a good sign. I know they're in there; I tracked Naomi all the way from the apartment and I saw her go in. Ostensibly to study with Betty for tort class.

She's been studying a lot, lately.

As my luck spirals, I keep looking more and more for signs. As harbingers of fate. On the sidewalk the entire way here I didn't step on a single crack. So, tonight is the night. The Feast of Stephen. Tonight, I'm looking for the sign — one way or the other — for what the future holds. If Naomi looks out the window — if she sees me down here on the sidewalk — if she stops what she's doing — If, if, if!

(Lights rise in the second-floor window.)

Ah, the floor show is about to begin. Anyone parked in a dark car or standing on the sidewalk looking up at the second-floor window can see it. Second floor, third window from the left.

(Two naked lesbian law student puppets, one short, one tall, appear, entwined.)

Naked lesbian law students. They'll make out like this for a long time, until Betty's law school work ethic pops up, stronger than their libidos: time to crack the books for tort class.

Naomi, I'm down here. I'm watching. Look down here, I'm down here.

(The lesbian law student puppets, still entwined, suddenly both read law books with a free hand while still necking.)

Once upon a time, I went through my own golden girl stage. I determined a long time ago that I would never again be a golden girl, but oh I could bed them. I still can't believe that I talked these girls into sleeping with me: tall, blue-eyed, blonde — the difference in height just spurred me on: as they stretched themselves down on the bed, they were a large canvas, and I a young Jackson Pollack, ready to fill every inch.

Naomi, Naomi, down here — I'm down here.

(The puppets make out more vigorously; in response:)

Okay; tonight will be the night that Naomi stops; she thinks for a moment, she remembers me and —

(Claire turns her attention to the window for a moment. The smaller puppet works her way down Betty's body.)

And she comes back to me ... Naomi ... For God's sake, stop ...

(Another puppet throe of love. The two puppets, entwined, tumble to the floor and out of sight. Suddenly, the light in the second floor, third window to the left, snaps off.)

Oh — oh that's not a good sign. I fear my Naomi has found her

45

golden girl.
(Beat.)

I am so very tired. I still wake on cue every four hours without an alarm; time to give Stephen his AZT. It would be about that time now.

And near the end with Stephen ... Fantastic pale lavenders and dark maroons ravaged the canvas of his skin until only his hands remained unchanged ... a young boy's hands ...
(The wind comes up.)

My hands are cold.
(Claire draws out mittens without fingertips and puts them on; she hesitates.)

There should be a word for me. "Cuck-old." Such an ugly sounding word. There should be a word for a female of the species.

I always imagined cuckolds murderous in a red hot rage, but it doesn't feel like that at all. It feels like inside it's snowing ...
(Claire sits there for a long moment. She reaches under her coat and brings out a revolver. Claire checks the ammunition and snaps the barrel closed.)

If she'd answered the door. If she'd looked down my way ... If I hadn't lost Naomi. If I'd kept Stephen alive. If If If ...
(The adult actor playing Stephen emerges into the shadows behind Claire and watches. Claire moves the gun up to her mouth, and closes her eyes. As she opens her mouth, the adult Stephen opens his mouth as well and blows his breath: we hear the spooky, amplified sound of breath — of a human sigh — that changes into the howl of winter wind. Claire opens her eyes. She lowers her gun. She listens, intently, to the wind. And then she rises, walking right by Stephen. She does not see him, and he watches her go.)
STEPHEN.

And as the air was cut by our father's hand.
WOMAN.

— Lovely Christmas —
MAN.

— Jesus —
REBECCA.

I will never have children!
CLAIRE.

— If If If If If!
STEPHEN.

— I will never strike a woman like that — !

46

(Woodblocks/percussion strike their discordant sounds, which seem to propel Stephen; he strides away from the car. As he rapidly walks around the stage to the door upstage, fifteen years in the future, a Japanese rock band plays a tune from the sixties — "Dancing Baby" — which we recognize as a version of "Good King Wenceslas."* In time to the music, Stephen pounds on the door. And pounds. He almost pants in rage. He pounds again.)

Open the Door!

Jesus Christ! Joe! Joe!

(Stephen pounds the door.)

You son of a bitch. I know you're in there. Open

(Pound.)

Up

(Pound.)

This goddamn door!

(Pound. Beat.)

You're in there with your little boyfriend. The one who just last year was an altar boy at St. Christopher's. The one who started shaving last month. The one who is so dewy-eyed that he believes all the bullshit you give him. I swear to god, you coward, that if you don't open up, I'm going to break this door down. I'll smash the lock.

(Yelling.)

JOE!

All of our neighbors in the entire Castro are listening to this little scene.

(To a neighbor next door:)

— Randy, I'm sorry I've disturbed you — please go back to the porno tapes you sit and watch in a stupor all night —

— Well, then, call the police.

Joe! You asswipe! That's real macho to sit inside, hiding behind your little boyfriend. I deserve the chance to talk to you, face to face.

(Pounds.)

I'm breaking through this door! I'll smash the glass!! Joe!

… He knows I won't break down the door. I restored this door — it's from the original house. 1897.

(Stephen strokes the wood.)

It's beautiful. Solid Oak.

(Stephen lays his hand flat on the wood.)

---

* See Special Note on Songs and Recordings on copyright page.

Oh; it's as warm as a young boy's hand.

It took me two days to strip the paint and get to the wood. I rubbed in the linseed oil by hand. And the glass — the beveled glass — all the windows in the house are original — 1897. Built by Fernando Nelson in the Stick/Eastlake style. I've stripped the floors, stripped the linoleum, restored the Lincrusta-Walton wainscoting — the former owner just tossed it away — it's amazing what people throw away.

(Beat.)

I like to sit on this porch and imagine the street as it must have been then. Clerks living next to bankers, cable car lines being laid beneath the cobblestones. San Francisco in its time was a bustling little Edo, a sister city to Kyoto.

Why do you suppose we so value antique houses when we toss away aging boyfriends?

I am aging. I was barely the age of that boy inside when Joe took up with me and now —

Oh, I've kept my girlish figure. But my skin … oh my skin … Mother always said a woman's age showed in her hands and her neck.

If only — if only I could just stop time.

Well. I'll never afford the Castro rents as a single working girl. It's back to the Tenderloin for me. Back to the walk up past the working girls on the street. Back —

(Sings.)

"Sometimes the cabin's gloomy, and the table's bare;
But then he'll kiss me and it's Christmas everywhere!
Troubles fly away and life is easy — go:"

— Joe! And whatever your name is, little boy: I wish you joy! Happiness! And eternal youth, if you have any brains to go with your wasp-thin waist. Medea gave such a splendid wedding gift to Jason's child bride: what gifts can I give?

I guess I'm leaving you the house! But there's a secret poison in this gift — the mortgage is in Joe's name.

Well, no sense in making a spectacle of yourself, Stephen.

(Stephen sits a moment.)

It does not matter. It does not matter. In ten years' time, all this will be forgotten.

(Stephen sits a moment; trying not to cry. But he does.)

He does not love me. He does not love me. Why does he not love me?

(Beat.)

In classical Japan it was poor form for an aristocrat to lose self-possession.

Hence arose the euphemism: "to wet one's sleeve on dew" which meant to wipe away one's tears.

(Stephen draws his sleeve across his eyes gracefully and wipes the tears.)

My sisters love to make fun of my adoration of all things Japanese. I've tried to enlighten them: books of Zeami, trips to see the imperial collection of screens and scrolls, performances of the Grand Kabuki — well! They still don't know their Kabuki from their Noh, and never will.

Time is a-wasting!

— Time to hoof yourself all over town to find a new beau.

(Stephen rises; from his back pocket he draws out a wool cap and puts it on.)

I say the night is still young — I'll go to the backroom at the Cave where the lights are low —

And hopefully in the dark I can forget how blue Joe's eyes are —

(Stephen strides across the stage to a bar: The Cave. Music gets louder.)

Ah. The Cave. Where my Prince Charming waits.

(Stephen walks to a spot where a puppet waits near the backroom of the Cave. The puppet is a very cute, hunky version of one of the Village People: leather vest, leather cap, and leather chaps.)

The music is mercifully loud. What?

(The puppet makes musical conversation.)

Never mind what my name is. It's — Antinous!

(The puppet can't hear over the noise.)

ANTINOUS!

Yes. An unusual name. It's Greek. I was named after a boy who was the beloved of an Emperor. The name of a very beautiful Greek boy

Whose beauty never aged.

I'm half-Greek. You can't tell in here, it's too dark to see. But I'm half-Greek

And half-Japanese.

(The puppet starts to "speak" —)

Oh, don't tell me your name! Just be a tall handsome stranger.

Yes, I'd like to. Very much. Wait. I can't see in the dark here —

What color are your eyes? I need to know.

(Puppet "speaks.")

Oh. Brown.

(Relieved.)

I love the color Brown! Dark brown eyes.

Great. That's enough of small talk! Let's do some big talk in the back room —

(Stephen and the puppet go into the back room; Stephen prepares to unzip himself. The puppet whispers a question. Stage whisper:)

No. A lady should always be prepared but — I must have left all my rubbers in my other purse —

(The puppet shrugs, "speaks.")

Okay. You don't have any either? Well, tant pis! Let's just —

(The puppet "Speaks" again. Raising his voice.)

— You know, this is hardly erotic foreplay! I'm a grown man, I know what's happening, I live in the *Castro*, for Christ's sake, and I don't want to talk about it — Screw It All! Do you want to do it, or shall I find another stud in the room in the next thirty seconds who will take care of business?

(The puppet shrugs, nods. Stephen talks to himself.)

I've always depended on the hardness of strangers …

(Stephen bends over à la Harvey Fierstein in Torch Song Trilogy. *Because I have personally never been in a back room. The puppet stands beside him; side by side they simulate a sexual act that means this play will never be performed in Texas.)*

Ready when you are.

(The puppet thrusts. On the first thrust, Stephen in pain:)

Oh!

(The second thrust: relaxation.)

Oh …

(The third thrust: pleasure.)

Ohhh …

(The fourth thrust: realization.)

Oh.

(Stephen straightens up; the puppet disappears. Stephen steps forward into the light. Stephen becomes the Ghost of Stephen; he talks to us.)

GHOST of STEPHEN.

— Oh! How my sisters will cry. I could feel the virus entering my body. But I could not undo what had been done.

And for the next several years, I could feel the virus multiply with a ferocious beauty — replicating patterns that changed and mutated.

I could not see the beauty then, of course. But I felt it take over and suckle my blood, diminishing the life inside me, striking the very cells.

It is a very terrible beauty. But it is a beauty all the same.

It takes distance to see the beauty in it. And now I have all the distance in the world.

As my grandmother would say: It's amazing what people throw away.

As the battle raged inside me, I had just enough time to think. I thought a lot about Ukiyo-E. The Floating World.

And while I was still strong enough, I would walk from my North Beach apartment to Japantown to study Sado — the Japanese Tea Ceremony.

I admired the bowl. I tried not to think. I contemplated the flowers. I tried not to think. I sipped the tea — I tried not to think.

And in the end, when the patterns of the virus dominated my blood as I struggled to breathe: I still remembered how blue Joe's eyes were.

No matter my efforts: I died just another white boy in San Francisco, dressed in silk, writing haiku to the fog.

(The Ghost walks in a circle. Other cast members enter and sing.)

I am granted a day each year to come back to the Floating World and observe it.

My spirit likes to walk along the bluffs of the Presidio at sunset. For those of you who can breathe, you can smell the dune grasses mixed with beach strawberry and primrose — an aphrodisia to the young men who comb the dunes and cliff for possibilities. They think I quicken my steps to turn in their direction, but they would only be half-right. I come to stand on the edge of the world and watch the spinning red orb of the sun race across the sky towards Japan.

I come back each year: on the waning of Christmas Day to the waning of the Feast of Stephen — my Feast Day.

All of our ancestors come back to observe the still breathing.

Those for whom time has not yet stopped.

You must feel our presence in the room at this time of day — the light has left the sky early. You sit at the table, drinking wine, laughing, enjoying the food.

But you shiver, too: and not against the cold outside.

You shiver because you feel our presence. More than each other. We watch you for a day. We are with you in the twilight.

And it is that time again: Christmas Day is passing into night.

I will walk upon the earth once more. I will visit my sisters as is my wont.

51

Now and then I drop in on Rebecca's little girl Grace; and I tiptoe into Stephen's room — Claire's son. My sisters' children are good children.

We've not yet come to the end of my sisters' stories, but when time stops for them, I'll be watching them too, as a member of a small and select audience.

But first I must take this year's journey.

I will meander along the bluffs until I find a man whose beauty is worth the trip back and I will borrow some of his breath. I must borrow some of his breath. He won't mind. The living have so much breath to give.

(The actor who plays the minister enters the stage. And oh, let him be beautiful.)

Ah.

Ukiyo-E!

(The minister/dancer will dance for Stephen. I do not pretend to understand the hayashi-goto of Noh: it is as unknown to me as the backroom of the bar. It is up to the director and the choreographer to interpret the mai-goto for western eyes. But let the dancer slowly, hypnotically come to life in the dance. And as the dance progresses, let the ghost become flesh — as the movement becomes stronger, and faster, the ghost of Stephen becomes angry with life. The dance should celebrate the beauty of this anger that drives the life-force in the young. I wrote this part to the musical segment "Porno 3003" by Happy End of the World, and a very manic version of "Tomorrow Shall be My Dancing Day." "This have I done for my True Love." At the end of the dance, the dancer is breathing hard. And right before the minister/dancer slips away again in shadow, he takes Stephen in his arms and pours his breath into Stephen's mouth. Stephen is left onstage, breathing hard from the dancer's breath.)

Ahh! My breath thunders in my chest! How wonderful it feels to breathe!

You cannot know how beautiful it is. When you are alive, you cannot see your breath.

But we your ancestors can see the air move when you breathe.

Your breathing creates a spectrum of color; the motion and heat of your life.

And often — in a church or a meeting, in a mosque — or like now, in a theatre

— Whenever and wherever you all gather together — then there are entire symphonies of air and color and light —

And whenever a family or an audience hold your breath together
— a moment of silence before you collectively expel the air —

Ah, then: Fireworks for the ancestors!

But of course, to see it, you must have the distance of the grave.

There is a moment I want you to watch with me. A moment of
time stopping.

You must come with me back in time.

Now, back to the back seat of the car. A tired and rusty
Rambler, that trudges

Through the ice and snow.

Come back with me now and perhaps you will see it.

*(The Ghost of Stephen circles around the stage and heads back into the
car where his sisters sit in the back, holding their puppets. His parents
sit still in the front seat, frozen in time. The Ghost of Stephen steps up
into the back between his sisters. Standing, he picks up the puppet of
Stephen. For a moment, the Ghost cradles the puppet in his arms. Then
the Ghost pours his breath into the puppet's mouth: The puppet
becomes animated. And then, the Ghost of Stephen becomes the puppeteer once more, and sits in the seat. He nods. The lights change again.
Stephen whispers to us.)*

Ukiyo-E!

*(The puppeteers stand and manipulate the man and the woman in the
front seat.)*

Our mother pressed herself against the window.

There was a sigh.

What's done cannot be undone.

And then she broke the silence:

WOMAN.

"Well. What a lovely Christmas you've given me."

CLAIRE.

And our father drew back his right hand:

MAN.

Je-Sus-Christt!

*(The puppeteers guide the man and woman in the front seat: the man
raises his right hand and backhands the woman, slowly, ritualistically.
Woodblocks strike.)*

REBECCA.

It's as if the car knew —

CLAIRE.

The car broke free, lurched and spun

GHOST of STEPHEN.

Our father pressed on the brake

REBECCA.

The car became a sled on the ice

(There are four sharp movements of their bodies in the car.)

CLAIRE.

Spinning off the road

It came to a stop

At the brink of a steep precipice.

GHOST of STEPHEN.

A sharp embankment over the creek

Known as Piney Branch.

REBECCA.

The metal of the car groaned

Toward the edge of the cliff.

Too dark to see the bottom of the creek bed

The car longed to join its steel with ice.

GHOST of STEPHEN.

We held our breath; we dared not breathe.

Would our father start the engine

Too quickly, slip on the accelerator

And send the car down the banks?

CLAIRE.

And then our mother spoke, loud enough

In the front seat to be heard throughout the car:

WOMAN.

You son of a bitch. You bastard. Go ahead. Kill us all,

You reckless bastard. Throw us all away.

MAN.

Don't. I'm warning you. Don't.

WOMAN.

You don't have the balls.

REBECCA.

For a moment no one dared to move.

The wind had come up.

Black air on blue snow.

Then Claire spoke from the back seat of the car.

CLAIRE.

I want to get out.

MAN.

Don't touch the door.

GHOST of STEPHEN.

The slightest movement would be all it would take to spin us down.

REBECCA.

Claire trembled in the back seat.

CLAIRE.

I want to get out.

MAN.

Stay in the car.

REBECCA.

Our sister made the slightest move towards the door.

CLAIRE.

I want —

MAN.

— Don't move!

(To the woman beside him.)

Tell your daughter to stay in the car.

WOMAN.

(With a strange laugh.)

My daughter must learn to look out for herself.

REBECCA.

For a moment, there was silence. And then Stephen
Stretched his arm towards his youngest sister.
He reached and took our arms in his.

(The puppeteers and puppets look at each other and lock arms.)

GHOST of STEPHEN.

And the fragile arms of the children
Linked, stretched and strained
And the thin strands of flesh
Did not break.

CLAIRE.

And in this moment in the balance
Our father bowed his head and prayed to a god he did not
    believe in.

MAN.

God. Let me start over. Let me take back this day.

WOMAN.

If I try harder — If I have another child —

MAN.

My children are good children —

WOMAN.

If I dress a bit younger — If I say softer things —

MAN.

My wife is … my wife.

WOMAN.

If —

MAN.

    If —

WOMAN.

        If —

MAN.

            If —

WOMAN and MAN.

If …

(Beat. The Narrators almost turn to each other.)

REBECCA.

And then our father thought of Sheila.

GHOST of STEPHEN.

The cream of her breasts

CLAIRE.

The sliver of her thighs

REBECCA.

And he wanted to see her.

He must see her.

CLAIRE.

Sheila —

REBECCA.

    — Sheila —

GHOST of STEPHEN.

        — Sheila.

CLAIRE.

We held our breath as father started the car.

Gentler than the touch of his fingers

On the thighs of his lover

REBECCA.

Gentler than his kiss on her brow

Our father pressed the pedal

And gently urged the car back

Away from the Piney Branch

CLAIRE.

And when at last we were safely away

From the edge
REBECCA.

As one family and one flesh,

We breathed as one:

ALL.

Ahhhhhh …

(Simultaneously, we hear again the amplified sound of breath that changes into the winter wind.)

GHOST of STEPHEN.

(To us.)

Ah! How beautiful! Do you see it?

(The Ghost of Stephen watches the currents of color and air. They sit motionless. Beat.)

And then our father turned and said to us:

MAN.

Children:

— let's go home.

GHOST of STEPHEN.

And so —

— we went.

(Suddenly, the puppeteers in the back seat crane their necks up into a beautiful shaft of light. Upon their upturned faces, it begins to snow.)

End of Play

PROPERTY LIST

Puppets
Small boxes
Miniature trees, wreaths, reindeer (STAGEHANDS)
Paper (STAGEHANDS)
Scarf (STAGEHANDS)
Mittens without fingertips (STAGEHANDS, CLAIRE)
Wool cap (STAGEHANDS, STEPHEN)
Box containing leather diary (REBECCA)
Soccer ball (STAGEHANDS)
Kites (STAGEHANDS)
Clothing (PUPPET)
Bench (STAGEHANDS)
Law books (PUPPETS)
Revolver (CLAIRE)

SOUND EFFECTS

Christmas melody, punctuated by sound of tire chain
Christmas music, in the tonality of Bunraku
Metallic pluck of the samisen
Wooden percussion
Japanese rock music
An amplified breath that turns into a moan of winter wind
Wind
Music

NEW PLAYS

★ **MONTHS ON END by Craig Pospisil.** In comic scenes, one for each month of the year, we follow the intertwined worlds of a circle of friends and family whose lives are poised between happiness and heartbreak. "...a triumph...these twelve vignettes all form crucial pieces in the eternal puzzle known as human relationships, an area in which the playwright displays an assured knowledge that spans deep sorrow to unbounded happiness." –*Ann Arbor News*. "...rings with emotional truth, humor...[an] endearing contemplation on love...entertaining and satisfying." –*Oakland Press*. [5M, 5W] ISBN: 0-8222-1892-5

★ **GOOD THING by Jessica Goldberg.** Brings us into the households of John and Nancy Roy, forty-something high-school guidance counselors whose marriage has been increasingly on the rocks and Dean and Mary, recent graduates struggling to make their way in life. "...a blend of gritty social drama, poetic humor and unsubtle existential contemplation..." –*Variety*. [3M, 3W] ISBN: 0-8222-1869-0

★ **THE DEAD EYE BOY by Angus MacLachlan.** Having fallen in love at their Narcotics Anonymous meeting, Billy and Shirley-Diane are striving to overcome the past together. But their relationship is complicated by the presence of Sorin, Shirley-Diane's fourteen-year-old son, a damaged reminder of her dark past. "...a grim, insightful portrait of an unmoored family..." –*NY Times*. "MacLachlan's play isn't for the squeamish, but then, tragic stories delivered at such an unrelenting fever pitch rarely are." –*Variety*. [1M, 1W, 1 boy] ISBN: 0-8222-1844-5

★ **[SIC] by Melissa James Gibson.** In adjacent apartments three young, ambitious neighbors come together to discuss, flirt, argue, share their dreams and plan their futures with unequal degrees of deep hopefulness and abject despair. "A work...concerned with the sound and power of language..." –*NY Times*. "...a wonderfully original take on urban friendship and the comedy of manners—a *Design for Living* for our times..." –*NY Observer*. [3M, 2W] ISBN: 0-8222-1872-0

★ **LOOKING FOR NORMAL by Jane Anderson.** Roy and Irma's twenty-five-year marriage is thrown into turmoil when Roy confesses that he is actually a woman trapped in a man's body, forcing the couple to wrestle with the meaning of their marriage and the delicate dynamics of family. "Jane Anderson's bittersweet transgender domestic comedy-drama ...is thoughtful and touching and full of wit and wisdom. A real audience pleaser." –*Hollywood Reporter*. [5M, 4W] ISBN: 0-8222-1857-7

★ **ENDPAPERS by Thomas McCormack.** The regal Joshua Maynard, the old and ailing head of a mid-sized, family-owned book-publishing house in New York City, must name a successor. One faction in the house backs a smart, "pragmatic" manager, the other faction a smart, "sensitive" editor and both factions fear what the other's man could do to this house— and to them. "If Kaufman and Hart had undertaken a comedy about the publishing business, they might have written *Endpapers*...a breathlessly fast, funny, and thoughtful comedy ...keeps you amused, guessing, and often surprised...profound in its empathy for the paradoxes of human nature." –*NY Magazine*. [7M, 4W] ISBN: 0-8222-1908-5

★ **THE PAVILION by Craig Wright.** By turns poetic and comic, romantic and philosophical, this play asks old lovers to face the consequences of difficult choices made long ago. "The script's greatest strength lies in the genuineness of its feeling." –*Houston Chronicle*. "Wright's perceptive, gently witty writing makes this familiar situation fresh and thoroughly involving." –*Philadelphia Inquirer*. [2M, 1W (flexible casting)] ISBN: 0-8222-1898-4

DRAMATISTS PLAY SERVICE, INC.
440 Park Avenue South, New York, NY 10016 212-683-8960 Fax 212-213-1539
postmaster@dramatists.com www.dramatists.com

NEW PLAYS

★ **BE AGGRESSIVE by Annie Weisman.** Vista Del Sol is paradise, sandy beaches, avocado-lined streets. But for seventeen-year-old cheerleader Laura, everything changes when her mother is killed in a car crash, and she embarks on a journey to the Spirit Institute of the South where she can learn "cheer" with Bible belt intensity. "...filled with lingual gymnastics...stylized rapid-fire dialogue..." –*Variety*. "...a new, exciting, and unique voice in the American theatre..." –*BackStage West*. [1M, 4W, extras] ISBN: 0-8222-1894-1

★ **FOUR by Christopher Shinn.** Four people struggle desperately to connect in this quiet, sophisticated, moving drama. "...smart, broken-hearted...Mr. Shinn has a precocious and forgiving sense of how power shifts in the game of sexual pursuit...He promises to be a playwright to reckon with..." –*NY Times*. "A voice emerges from an American place. It's got humor, sadness and a fresh and touching rhythm that tell of the loneliness and secrets of life...[a] poetic, haunting play." –*NY Post*. [3M, 1W] ISBN: 0-8222-1850-X

★ **WONDER OF THE WORLD by David Lindsay-Abaire.** A madcap picaresque involving Niagara Falls, a lonely tour-boat captain, a pair of bickering private detectives and a husband's dirty little secret. "Exceedingly whimsical and playfully wicked. Winning and genial. A top-drawer production." –*NY Times*. "Full frontal lunacy is on display. A most assuredly fresh and hilarious tragicomedy of marital discord run amok...absolutely hysterical..." –*Variety*. [3M, 4W (doubling)] ISBN: 0-8222-1863-1

★ **QED by Peter Parnell.** Nobel Prize-winning physicist and all-around genius Richard Feynman holds forth with captivating wit and wisdom in this fascinating biographical play that originally starred Alan Alda. "QED is a seductive mix of science, human affections, moral courage, and comic eccentricity. It reflects on, among other things, death, the absence of God, travel to an unexplored country, the pleasures of drumming, and the need to know and understand." –*NY Magazine*. "Its rhythms correspond to the way that people—even geniuses—approach and avoid highly emotional issues, and it portrays Feynman with affection and awe." –*The New Yorker*. [1M, 1W] ISBN: 0-8222-1924-7

★ **UNWRAP YOUR CANDY by Doug Wright.** Alternately chilling and hilarious, this deliciously macabre collection of four bedtime tales for adults is guaranteed to keep you awake for nights on end. "Engaging and intellectually satisfying...a treat to watch." –*NY Times*. "Fiendishly clever. Mordantly funny and chilling. Doug Wright teases, freezes and zaps us." –*Village Voice*. "Four bite-size plays that bite back." –*Variety*. [flexible casting] ISBN: 0-8222-1871-2

★ **FURTHER THAN THE FURTHEST THING by Zinnie Harris.** On a remote island in the middle of the Atlantic secrets are buried. When the outside world comes calling, the islanders find their world blown apart from the inside as well as beyond. "Harris winningly produces an intimate and poetic, as well as political, family saga." –*Independent (London)*. "Harris' enthralling adventure of a play marks a departure from stale, well-furrowed theatrical terrain." –*Evening Standard (London)*. [3M, 2W] ISBN: 0-8222-1874-7

★ **THE DESIGNATED MOURNER by Wallace Shawn.** The story of three people living in a country where what sort of books people like to read and how they choose to amuse themselves becomes both firmly personal and unexpectedly entangled with questions of survival. "This is a playwright who does not just tell you what it is like to be arrested at night by goons or to fall morally apart and become an aimless yet weirdly contented ghost yourself. He has the originality to make you feel it." –*Times (London)*. "A fascinating play with beautiful passages of writing..." –*Variety*. [2M, 1W] ISBN: 0-8222-1848-8

DRAMATISTS PLAY SERVICE, INC.
440 Park Avenue South, New York, NY 10016 212-683-8960 Fax 212-213-1539
postmaster@dramatists.com www.dramatists.com

NEW PLAYS

★ **SHEL'S SHORTS by Shel Silverstein.** Lauded poet, songwriter and author of children's books, the incomparable Shel Silverstein's short plays are deeply infused with the same wicked sense of humor that made him famous. "…[a] childlike honesty and twisted sense of humor." –*Boston Herald.* "…terse dialogue and an absurdity laced with a tang of dread give [*Shel's Shorts*] more than a trace of Samuel Beckett's comic existentialism." –*Boston Phoenix.* [flexible casting] ISBN: 0-8222-1897-6

★ **AN ADULT EVENING OF SHEL SILVERSTEIN by Shel Silverstein.** Welcome to the darkly comic world of Shel Silverstein, a world where nothing is as it seems and where the most innocent conversation can turn menacing in an instant. These ten imaginative plays vary widely in content, but the style is unmistakable. "…[*An Adult Evening*] shows off Silverstein's virtuosic gift for wordplay…[and] sends the audience out…with a clear appreciation of human nature as perverse and laughable." –*NY Times.* [flexible casting] ISBN: 0-8222-1873-9

★ **WHERE'S MY MONEY? by John Patrick Shanley.** A caustic and sardonic vivisection of the institution of marriage, laced with the author's inimitable razor-sharp wit. "…Shanley's gift for acid-laced one-liners and emotionally tumescent exchanges is certainly potent…" –*Variety.* "…lively, smart, occasionally scary and rich in reverse wisdom." –*NY Times.* [3M, 3W] ISBN: 0-8222-1865-8

★ **A FEW STOUT INDIVIDUALS by John Guare.** A wonderfully screwy comedy-drama that figures Ulysses S. Grant in the throes of writing his memoirs, surrounded by a cast of fantastical characters, including the Emperor and Empress of Japan, the opera star Adelina Patti and Mark Twain. "Guare's smarts, passion and creativity skyrocket to awesome heights…" –*Star Ledger.* "…precisely the kind of good new play that you might call an everyday miracle…every minute of it is fresh and newly alive…" –*Village Voice.* [10M, 3W] ISBN: 0-8222-1907-7

★ **BREATH, BOOM by Kia Corthron.** A look at fourteen years in the life of Prix, a Bronx native, from her ruthless girl-gang leadership at sixteen through her coming to maturity at thirty. "…vivid world, believable and eye-opening, a place worthy of a dramatic visit, where no one would want to live but many have to." –*NY Times.* "…rich with humor, terse vernacular strength and gritty detail…" –*Variety.* [1M, 9W] ISBN: 0-8222-1849-6

★ **THE LATE HENRY MOSS by Sam Shepard.** Two antagonistic brothers, Ray and Earl, are brought together after their father, Henry Moss, is found dead in his seedy New Mexico home in this classic Shepard tale. "…His singular gift has been for building mysteries out of the ordinary ingredients of American family life…" –*NY Times.* "…rich moments …Shepard finds gold." –*LA Times.* [7M, 1W] ISBN: 0-8222-1858-5

★ **THE CARPETBAGGER'S CHILDREN by Horton Foote.** One family's history spanning from the Civil War to WWII is recounted by three sisters in evocative, intertwining monologues. "…bittersweet music—[a] rhapsody of ambivalence…in its modest, garrulous way…theatrically daring." –*The New Yorker.* [3W] ISBN: 0-8222-1843-7

★ **THE** ⟨…⟩ d heartbreaking
homage ⟨…⟩ ⟨…⟩ and doesn't let
them out ⟨…⟩ a delightful rev-
elation o⟨…⟩ ece of lingering
beauty." ⟨…⟩ 222-1891-7

<blockquote>
PLAY #1113

Vogel, Paula.

The long Christmas ride home
</blockquote>

DRAMATISTS PLAY SERVICE, INC.
440 Park Avenue South, New York, NY 10016 212-683-8960 Fax 212-213-1539
postmaster@dramatists.com www.dramatists.com